Timmy Climbs Higher

Timmy Climbs Higher

Rose Stilwell
Illustrator Hannah Sierra

Book 3 of 3 - How Timmy Grew Series

Copyright

Timmy Climbs Higher
Book 3 of 3 - How Timmy Grew Series

This educational book offers guidance as children grow and begin school based on a fictional account. The events and characters herein are imaginary, do not refer to specific places or persons.
The opinions expressed in this manuscript are solely the opinions of the author and do not represent those of the publisher. The author has represented and warranted ownership and/or legal right to publish all the materials in this book.
Timmy Climbs Higher
All Rights Reserved.
Copyright © 2022 Rose Stilwell V-1.0
This book may not be reproduced, transmitted, or stored in whole or in part by any means, including graphic, electronic, or mechanical without the express written consent of the publisher except brief quotations embodied in critical articles and reviews.
Nova Publishing, Bakersfield, California

Dedication

I thought a lot about this before I began to write. Who would I dedicate this series to? My family or friends from the past who had loved me and helped me to grow. My wonderful family and friends I am blessed to have now. Then I made my decision. Each one has been a part of my life and I can leave no one out. So, my dearly beloved, who have helped me be the person that I am, I dedicate it to all of you with my love!

Table of Contents

1	California Fun	Page 1
2	A Special Time	Page 3
3	A New Beginning	Page 5
4	Not Very Funny	Page 7
5	One Step Up	Page 9
6	Homeroom Together	Page 11
7	Separate Ways	Page 14
8	Struggles Continue	Page 15
9	Together Again	Page 17
10	Physical Education	Page 19
11	Study Hall	Page 22
12	Another Step	Page 25
13	Growing Up	Page 28
14	Listen and Learn	Page 30

15	Study It All	Page 32
16	A Year To Remember	Page 35
17	Summertime	Page 37
18	We Begin Again	Page 41
19	Moving Along	Page 44
20	Living And Learning	Page 50
21	Friends Together	Page 54
22	High School	Page 57
23	Three Young Men	Page 58
24	A Giant Step	Page 60
25	School Year Nine	Page 61
26	Not Alone!	Page 63
27	Cafeteria Lunch	Page 65
28	First Day Ends	Page 66
29	Story Continues	Page 68
30	Smooth Sailing	Page 71

31	Next Semester	Page 73
32	Auto or Train	Page 75
33	Return Again	Page 77
34	Looking	Page 82
35	Junior Year	Page 85
36	Prom Night	Page 87
37	Flying High	Page 90
38	Senior Year - Never An End	Page 93
39	GRADUATION	Page 96
	EPILOGUE	Page 100
	My Thank You	Page 102

Preface

Thank you for returning to learn more about Timmy. Perhaps, as we read about his climb up the ladder to adulthood, we will learn more about ourselves. This fictional child is blessed with a wonderful set of parents. I wish I had been as understanding and as great a parent as they were.

Looking back will never help you. Just as Timmy moves on with life, so must we. Timmy's struggles, his happiness, and sometimes sorrow will make him a stronger person. Let's watch Timmy together as he climbs the ladder of life. If Timmy were real, he would send you a hug and a big smile. Read on!

Chapter One

California Fun

I could never decide if this summer was longer or shorter than the ones before. I wanted it to be longer so it wouldn't be time to go back to school. I had always loved school, but this would be different from anything I had done before.

Different schools, different students, and lots of different teachers. Will it be a struggle or a happy time? As the day grew closer, I was getting worried!

However, summer is always fun. My best friend Jimmy and my family traveled together again in our rented RVs. We traveled the California coastline and stopped at many different towns. Our first stop was Morro Bay where we saw Morro Rock and fished off the pier. Later we had a great dinner of fish and chips. We stayed there two days and visited the many shops.

Our moms loved the antique shops and made a lot of purchases. While they shopped, our dads and Jimmy and I walked on the beach and looked for shells or artifacts.

Jimmy found a gorgeous conch shell and I found a gold ring! Jimmy's mom got the shell, and my mom got the gold ring. What a blessing to be a giver instead of always a receiver.

Our parents decided we would travel down the coast and visit San Diego and the large zoo there. It was super great! We visited Monterey, Santa Monica, and many other cities. One of the many tours we took was to Hearst Castle in San Simeon. The main house has 115 rooms.

I couldn't imagine living in a house like that. You had to go on a tour. You could not just walk around by yourself. I heard dad tell mom that these tours were very costly so that better be our last one that summer.

Chapter Two

A Special Time

Before we went home, we went to a town that was special to my mom. A great place was Santa Cruz! We had heard about her going there with her family when she was a child and how many good memories she had of their times together. I could understand why it was special when we got there.

There were so many different rides along the boardwalk, some new and some older. We saw The Giant Dipper, one of the oldest wooden roller coasters in the nation. We did not ride that one!

Mom was a little disappointed because the giant slide had been taken down. She told us how you would climb up the stairs to the top, put a gunny sack down, sit on it and slide down about two stories.

A wonderful memory to share. I was only beginning to understand what our parents were doing for us every summer. They were helping us create our own memories to share with others! Our three weeks were finished, and we went home tired and very happy.

The next few weeks we went shopping for school clothes and worried about school. We bought backpacks and worried. We learned where the bus stop was and worried.

Our moms caught on and they each bought a fish (not real) on a wooden board. Every time you walked by it would sing the song, DON'T WORRY, BE HAPPY, and wiggle. My dad said, "that fish has never been here before and he is happy and singing. If it works for him, it will work for you. You are blessed to live in a country where you can go to school. It is not like that in many places in the world. So, count your blessings and enjoy your time in Jr. High."

Chapter Three

A New Beginning

Well, here I am again! Getting ready to start school all over. This is going to be a little different because as you already know, (this is a joke) I am super smart.

I guess I am doing ok because my grades are pretty good. I love to read and am a good reader. My favorites are comic books and dog stories. Books about horses are good too.

Let's look back a little. I have great loving parents and I have my best friend, Jimmy. My life has been blessed to have these advantages. But inside, I am not so sure about me and junior high.

Math is not only my worst subject, but it keeps getting harder. Adding, subtracting, and even multiplication are fine. I have had a little trouble with division. It was fine until we began long division. Borrow, carry, and all that stuff – it was hard!

Once again, my dad came through. Many nights, as I struggled, dad quietly showed me the steps over and over again. I always said, "Thank you dad for your help." Although dad never knew, I sometimes shed tears as I lay on my bed, knowing I still did not get it.

Then one day it happened! It was like a light bulb went off in my head. As the teacher was going over a problem on the chalkboard, I caught on. That is what dad has been telling me! I could have shouted, but I didn't. I could hardly wait to get home and tell him.

You should have seen his face and his great big smile. He hugged me and then mom came into the room and asked what was happening. I told her and got another big hug. "This calls for a celebration, he said. After dinner, we'll go get some ice cream."

Chapter Four

Not Very Funny

My parents still think I am super smart. They are also proud that I have good manners and respect for others. Sometimes it is hard not to laugh out loud when I probably shouldn't. Let me tell you a story that happened in sixth grade.

I am sure we all remember that there is always a class clown. One day we had a substitute teacher. She was a little older than most teachers are. The clown walked into the room with a smile. The teacher said, "your work is on the board, please sit down and get started."

Very loudly and with a grin on his face he said, "ok grandma!" No one laughed as he had expected. The words had barely left his mouth when the teacher responded. "I am not your grandmother and would not want to be a grandmother of a boy who is as rude as you are." There was complete silence as we filed in and took our seats. There was not a peep out of anyone the rest of the day unless we were answering a question the teacher asked. The clown looked a little sheepish as he left the room. I silently applauded the teacher for her fantastic response. I'll bet that boy's parents never heard that story!

Moving along, I am feeling a little scared of junior high. I have only had one teacher each year and now I would have many. What if one of them didn't like me or I didn't like him or her" Once again, time marches on.

Chapter Five

One Step Up

As Jimmy and I walked to the corner to wait for the school bus, I think both of us were a little worried. We didn't say much, but we did not look like two happy campers.

I finally broke the silence by saying, "are you scared?" My friend looked at me and said, "yes!"

We had always been in the same class and now we would have six classes every day. Would we have the same ones? Who knew?

Our parents had told us we would love Jr. High School. Our friends who were a little older told us the same thing. However, they had already been there, and we hadn't! Suddenly Jimmy said, "Remember what Mrs. Scott said, we have to climb the ladder."

Then, I spoke these words, "one thing we do know, we are both super smart!" Remember the fish we said, and we both laughed and stepped onto the bus. We were beginning a new chapter in our lives.

Chapter Six

Homeroom Together

The only thing we knew was the number of our homeroom. We knew we had that class together, but it was the only one we were sure of. We were to learn about our other classes that morning.

Our instructor, (teacher), started the morning like every school day with the Pledge of Allegiance. After we were seated, he called each student's name and gave them their schedule of classes.

The room was quiet for a few minutes as we looked at them. The instructor explained that the following semester we would have a choice of several different classes. This semester we had Math, English, Science, P.E. Social Studies, Music and one study hall class to work on homework or unfinished schoolwork.

"Make no mistake," he said, it is STUDY HALL, NOT PLAY TIME! That was pretty cool.

He went on to tell us he would be our English instructor, and this would be our homeroom. Being very strict, he told us what he expected from the students in his classroom. Then he said in a loud voice, "you got that!" AND, then he laughed!

"Have I scared you enough?" he said with a smile on his face. "I am glad that is over, now let's be friends. My name is Mr. Smith and if you just do your work, pay attention and act like Jr. High students should, we will all be happy."

His next comments were "I see all of you brought your backpacks, and you will need them because the books are heavy. I will pass them out tomorrow.

Now I will show you your lockers where you may keep them when not needed. Every student will have one with a combination padlock." We each chose a locker, and the padlocks had a tag with the combination and instructions on it.

We opened them and placed the tag in our backpacks. Then the bell rang and each one of us struggled to find their next class.

I was a very exciting first day. We had plenty stories to tell our Moms and Dads.

Chapter Seven

Separate Ways

As we left our homeroom, we parted ways for the first time in our school days. I had no idea what lay ahead that first day. That was hard enough, but of course you can guess what my next class was…MATH! Timmy's and my classes were different, as students were placed by skill level. I felt in my heart that this was going to be a bad day. Then I thought about what my dad had said that I was blessed to live in a country where I could go to school. Thinking about that raised my spirits and I walked into the room with a smile on my face, ready to start climbing again.

Chapter Eight

Struggles Continue

My next stop was room 22. As I walked in, I saw several kids that I knew. That helped a little! One of the boys was David and one of the girls was Eudora. David had become a friend and Eudora was cuter all the time!
Back to the class! We sat down wherever we wanted to.

Of course, David, Eudora, and I sat close together. Everyone was getting acquainted and talking until the instructor entered the room. Immediately the noise ceased.

She introduced herself as Miss Stein. She told us a little bit about her time as a teacher. She had taught at this school for five years and it was a great school! "All the instructors are very nice," she said, "I think you will enjoy your time here."

"I would like two boys to pass out the math books. Who would like to do this?"

We, David, and I quickly volunteered. We passed out the large books and others passed out the workbooks. Time to get to work!

As we listened to our instructor, I was already getting confused. What was she talking about I thought? I had never been so confused about math. You know it has always been difficult for me.

Why are there always new kinds of math? Miss Stein began telling us what we would be working on this semester. WOW!

Let me tell you a few! Number sense and operations, algebra, geometry and spatial sense, ratio and proportional relationships, data analysis, and probability! We will talk about all these later she told us as we have the whole year to learn them. Easy for her to say!

Miss Stein then told us to read the first selection in the math book and complete the pages in the workbook. This took the rest of the period.

Chapter Nine

Together Again

Jimmy was waiting for me when class was over so we could walk together to our PE class.

"Wow," I said. "I don't know about your math class, but mine was hard!" Jimmy's reply was, "you can count on me to help you. We will start tonight." Then he said, "Before we begin, we will pray that you will understand math better." Could anyone have a better friend?

We walked on to the next class which we were having together. We talked about this strange new world we were entering in. I feel so unsure I said and a little frightened. I was already worried I would not remember the combination of my locker padlock! Jimmy laughed! "Remember the fish," he said. "You have the tag that came off the padlock in your backpack with the number on it." Then we both laughed!

"I wonder what we will do in PE?" said Jimmy. I wasn't too worried about it I thought. "Probably have fun," I said. I guess we will find out after lunch we told each other. And we did.

Chapter Ten

Physical Education

Two friends, Jimmy and I walked into our new class, happy to be together again. We were excited to see our new teacher. We thought he would be tall and muscular and very nice.

Surprise, surprise! We walked into the gym and were met by a small lady, about 5′ 3″ tall. We looked at each other and the other boys. They were probably thinking the same thing we were. Are we in the right place?

"Well," she said. "I guess you were not expecting me. My name is Miss Roberts, and I am your instructor. Please do not think that because I am a woman that I will be easy on you! You will probably wish you had a man teacher before this semester is over!

I am tough but willing to help you succeed in this class. My dad was a PE instructor and taught me how to be fair and always be understanding."

She told us she would take roll first and try to learn our names. This could take a while as she had four other classes.

"Let's talk about what your activities will be this semester.

First you will be graded on your participation, that is very important. We cannot always win but we can try hard!"

I will say one thing about Miss Roberts, she was tough! Our first task in PE was to run around the track. As it was hot outside, she had a bottle of water waiting for each of us and asked us to sit until we cooled off.

Then it was what she called warm up exercises. And we did warm up.

We spent the rest of the class listening while she told us what we would be doing in PE this year.

We would be playing inside the gym until the weather cooled off. This would include fitness training, basketball, and volleyball. We would not only play these games, but we would have to know the rules and would be tested on them.

She told us it would be a fun class but not always easy. Jimmy and I agreed we were anxious to see what we could learn and prove it with Miss Roberts tests. And made a kind of challenge between us to see who got the highest score.

Chapter Eleven

Study Hall

We left P.E. and continued our first day in seventh grade. We walked together to study hall and talked about our classes. As we entered, the classroom was almost full, but we found two seats together.

Everyone was talking about the first day and then the bell rang. Silence filled the air and then the instructor walked in.

An elderly man walked in with a smile on his face. "Welcome to our school, I think you will be happy here," he said. I have been here for twenty years, and I still love it! My name is Mr. Arnold, and I am here to help you."

Help us, I thought to myself. I wonder if he is good in math. Aren't we supposed to work on our own and finish our class work and homework. Then he explained.

The first thing I will help you with is the rules for this class. You are not here to play or visit with each other, but to do your work. There may be situations where two students may help each other. BUT, only with my permission. I will be available to help when I can.

Then he asked, "are there any questions?" One boy raised his hand and asked, "what do we do today, we don't have any work to do?" Mr. Arnold said, "we are just going to learn a little about each other. How did you like your first day here?"

A girl raised her hand and said, "I was scared and I still am. It is so different here, I see many new faces and I have a hard time finding my next class," she said, with the tears running down her cheeks.

"What is your name child," said the instructor. She replied in a soft voice, "Amy." "That is a lovely name, I have a granddaughter named Amy. Please look around and see if you know someone in this room,"

"Yes," she said, "I see Beth over on the other side of the room." "Excellent!" said Mr. Arnold. "Would everyone please stand and see if they have a friend in the room."

"Everyone please go to the outside isle and wait for instructions." "Amy and Beth, please find a seat together and sit down."

This was unbelievable! Slowly, he pointed to the next student standing and asked the question, do you see friends in this room? If the answer was yes, they took a seat together.

If the answer was no, Mr. Arnold would ask the class who would like to be a friend with this student, and they were seated together.

Everyone left this class with a new look at this school.

There were instructors and students who really cared about each other. We left with a clearer eyesight into this new school and an uplifted spirit and hope for success.

Love doesn't always have to be spoken; it can just be felt. With a smile on everyone's face, we went to the next class.

Chapter Twelve

Another Step

After the first day, I felt a little less out of place in the classroom. Have you ever felt like that? A little out of place. You don't know anyone in the room, and many have already found a friend.

No one says hi and you feel so alone. And then, someone says, "hey buddy, come and sit by me, I don't know anyone here." The loneliness slips away and the day looks brighter! Remembering that makes me look to help someone else feel they are not alone.

I still remember John. He came to our homeroom about two weeks after school had started. He wasn't dressed too nice and didn't raise his head to look at anyone.

Lonely and lost, a new school, no friends, and starting late. He left the class the same way he had come in, not looking at anyone.

I remembered loneliness and I caught him just outside the door. I gave him a light tap on the shoulder and said, "My name is

Timmy, what is yours?" He looked a little startled and then said, "John."

"What's your next class," I asked. John said, "It is math, and I am not good in math, and I do not like it." I started to laugh, "Join the club," I said. I told him I felt the same way, but I was trying. Then John told me this, "I used to try, but I really don't anymore.

My family never stays in one place very long, and that makes it hard to catch up. I hope this will be different as my dad went to trade school and learned to be a welder. He has been offered a good job in this town and he said we were going to settle down and stay here.

I hope so! I would like to have a friend.

I didn't say it, but I thought you have found two and haven't met the other one yet. This was the beginning of a friendship that would last many years. We became the three Musketeers.

His family bought a home and John became a different boy. Happy, smiling and he even began to try hard to learn math. I think I took a step up that day to being a better person myself.

Chapter Thirteen

Growing Up

How can I tell you all about my seventh-grade year? I look back at it as a big step in my growing up. My schoolwork was part of this, as I grew in knowledge. There are so many memories I want to share with you, but there was one life changing.

I told you that we always went to church on Sunday as a family. There came a special Sunday for me that year. It was the Sunday before Easter. I had heard about the Lord and salvation many times. That Sunday I listened carefully to the pastor as he spoke. Was he talking to me? Was he talking about me?

I grew a little uncomfortable and I knew there was something I needed in my life. As the invitation was given, I knew what I needed. It was the Lord Jesus. As I accepted Him as my Lord and Savior, my life was complete. I had a forever future. I was baptized on the next Sunday which was Easter. I was so happy I cried. My mom and dad cried too. I went back to school with a prayer in my heart and a desire for everyone to know Jesus.

Chapter Fourteen

Listen And Learn

Was seventh grade a turning point in my life? It was. I began to understand better that if you wanted to learn something, you needed to listen. This helped me in all my classes, especially math. As I struggled to listen, I also felt free to ask questions. I did not care if someone laughed at me or teased me at recess about a dumb question I had asked. I was ready to learn. AND math got better! You might say that I had a better teacher. You might say that I received more help that year. My answer would be that you were correct. However, I grew up to see that if I applied myself, listened, tried harder and not be a quitter, I could do better.

This was not only some help in math, but in every subject. I became better in my classwork and in my life. I began to see that it is not always me, me, me. Sometimes you can help a friend by listening to them. They just need someone to talk to.

Back to school, it became what my friends and family had said. I would love it and I did.

Chapter Fifteen

Study It All

I needed to check my schedule again. Is today the day I go to Science or Social Studies? We go to Science two days a week and Social Studies three. I guess I will get used to this new schedule. I did have a few classes with my friends, but I was not sure if this was one of them. The first week I seemed to feel the first day fear!!

This is still Monday, and I have Science. Happy Day! I walked into the room and there were two friends, Jimmy, and John. Both came up to me and then looked at one another. I smiled and said, I am very happy to see two friends in my class. Then I introduced them, and they shook hands, like men do.

There was already a lady at the desk, but the bell hadn't rung yet, so we talked together a little. Not a voice was heard after the bell rang and the lady stood up. WOW! I might have been only twelve, but I knew when a lady was gorgeous.

She introduced herself as Mrs. Blake and that this was her second-year teaching. She told us we would be learning about earth movements, seasons, planets and much more and how gravity holds it all together. This did not sound too hard, and we would study it all.

Mrs. Blake was a teacher! She not only knew what she was talking about, but she knew how to teach it. This is a talent that not all teachers have. Knowing about something and teaching about something are two different skills.

This was a great first week of seventh grade. OH! I forgot to mention lunch. The day would not be complete without talking about lunch in the cafeteria. I did say study it all didn't I? I almost did not know where to start as there were so many different items. Jimmy, John and I were together at lunch and everyone chose spaghetti, a roll, salad, and milk. And of course, a cookie.

The first day soon became a week, a month, and then a year. I cannot tell you what my favorite subject was as I liked them all. Well, almost all! I did come up a little in math. I got my first C. I will keep trying!! I remember what my dad said, "never give up!" And I won't.

Chapter Sixteen

A Year To Remember

What began in kindergarten continued. Another year at school completed and all were great. New teachers, new classes, and new friends. I will always remember these school days and I will never forget my friends.

Jimmy and I had been together throughout it all. We had many friends and I felt like we now had a special one in John. I told my parents about John, and they went to visit the family to get acquainted. They soon became friends. It was not long until all three families were having a picnic together at Jimmy's house. Seventh grade was over, and it was vacation time. What will we do this summer?

As our families continued to get better acquainted, there were many discussions. Our parents talked together, John and Jimmy and I talked together. Then one night after dinner we all talked together. Our parents said we would sleep on it and decide later as we had plenty of time to think.

Chapter Seventeen

Summertime

No school, no work, and no place to go. Our dad's vacations would be later this year. Their time off would be in July. That seemed hard. We did not have long to wait. All three of us were going to church camp. It started next week!

John, Jimmy, and I were leaving Monday. We would be traveling in the church bus to a site in the mountains. I do not know when I have had such a great time. I was grateful for the swimming lessons where I learned how to swim.

We swam, fished, hiked, played sports, and ate delicious food. One day we went horseback riding. Now let me tell you the best part. Every night after dinner we sat by a campfire and had Bible study.

The talks were, of course, about our Lord Jesus Christ. There were boys at camp that did not know how the Son of God came to earth and offered salvation to the world. There were many that went to church and knew about Jesus but had not accepted Him as their Savior.

At night when we were in our sleeping bags we talked about the service. Jimmy and I had already accepted Jesus and John wanted to know more about our experience.

We answered as well as we could and prayed with him. During that week, twenty-five boys accepted Christ as Savior. The first one to step out was John! So much joy, so many tears, so many smiles and so many hugs.

The bus ride home was filled with boys singing along, singing our songs, side by side.

July was finally here and once again, our families had vacation planned. There was a difference this time, there were three motorhomes.

We spent one week at the California beaches. We went to Disneyland and had a great time! Our last trip was to Catalina Island. This is a fantastic place to play at the beach in the harbor, and hike and explore all the trials above the town.

When I was chewing gum, I never thought about the man who actually was the maker of this great vacation place. I am going to share something I read about Catalina.

THE WRIGLEY VISION

"In 1919, chewing gum entrepreneur William Wrigley Jr. bought nearly every share of the Santa Catalina Island Company until he owned a controlling interest. He then invested millions in his vision to create a "playground for all" on Catalina Island, building infrastructure, a reservoir, Hotel Atwater, Bird Park, and other attractions."

Can you imagine all this from a pack of gum?

Chapter Eighteen

We Begin Again

A new school year and our last year at this school. How time flies! Once again, we rode the bus together, but there were three of us this time. We had a good laugh as we told John about the fish. BE HAPPY, DON'T WORRY.

We said that would be our motto this year. It was good to be back. We were ready to climb a little higher. We were confident in our ability to succeed.

And then we went to our homeroom! Once again, the first period was English. As we laughed and talked until the bell rang, we had no idea what the morning would bring.

As the bell rang, our instructor came through the door. She was an elderly lady who introduced herself as Mrs. Terrible, My mistake! I mean Mrs. Terry. Let's get right to work," she said.

"You are here to keep up with the assignments and follow my instructions. Your first assignment is this. Tomorrow you will bring in a poem that you have written. Please do not make any mistakes in grammar. You may have the rest of the period to begin."

What a way to start a new year! As we left the class, we thought she was Mrs. Terrible Terry. I know, that was not very nice.

Then we remembered the fish and we laughed together again as we parted ways to go to our next class. We all had math but only John and I were together. Both of us still struggled with math. I had shared with John what my dad had told me, You Never Give Up.

We walked into class willing to keep trying. We were blessed to have a kind, supportive teacher who worked hard to help us understand more about math. And it began to sink in. Maybe I can do this I thought to myself. Then I said a little prayer.

The day went well, our instructors were nice, and we mostly talked about what we would learn in each class and what was expected of us. We were pleased with the day but a little worried about the poem for first period.

Chapter Nineteen

Moving Along

There were three pretty quiet boys on the bus the next morning. I asked if they had their poems and they said yes. We didn't talk about it again and instead talked about our other classes.

We all liked our teachers, except Mrs. Terry. She just seemed kind of cold towards us kids. We walked with the other students into her class. There she sat, calmly waiting for us to quiet down, Then the bell rang.

"Who would like to read their poem first?" she said. Not a hand was raised. Then, out of the clear blue sky she said, "Timmy please come to the front of the room and read your poem."

I didn't look at her. I just wanted to sink under my desk.

"Now please," she said more loudly.

I stood up as tall as I possibly could and walked to the front and began to read.

MY DOG FRED

I had a dog,

His name was Fred.

The only trick he knew,

Was how to play dead.

Training Fred wasn't easy,

It made me feel a little queasy.

I did not know what to do,

It had me in a stew!

I woke him up,

With this one thing,

I pulled a bone

By his nose on a string.

Fred sat up and begged,

Even stood upon one leg.

And that was the end,

Of Fred playing dead!

You will not believe what happened next, it was amazing. Mrs. Terry started to laugh, then everyone laughed. From that moment on we recognized that Mrs. Terry wasn't terrible, she was just a lady that could be both stern and nice and we began to respect her. Before the year was over, she was one of our favorite teachers!

My poem was not the only one that brought a laugh. Jimmies was very short.

MY NAME

I don't know how to write a poem,

I don't know how to write a song.

I do know how to write my name,

But it's boring,

It always looks the same!

I cannot say that John's poem was funny. It was fantastic! One of the very best!!!

A LITTLE BEAR

A little bear has lost his way
I wonder where,
He was before today.
He looks so sad,
I wish I could help.
When I tried to help,
He let out a yelp.
He turned and ran,
And I hope I am right,
I saw something,
That gave me a fright.
I think it was his mom,
She looked big and hairy.
I will say, that to me,
She looked pretty scary.
They lumbered away,
Together again.
I felt for a moment,
I could have been their friend.
The scripture says,
A lion will lay down with a lamb,
Perhaps in heaven,
I will see them again.

I might as well tell you about the best poem in the class. It was written by a girl named Rose.

TOYS

Last night I was frightened,
And it wasn't a dream,
From somewhere close,
I heard a loud scream.
I looked carefully around,
There was nothing to see.
Only Raggedy Ann,
Lying close beside me.
She looked somehow different,
Her mouth opened wide.
A toy curled up beside her,
And close to her side.
It was my favorite stuffed toy,
Which was only a bear.
I laughed out loud,
As I placed him on a chair.
Was it really a scream?
Or was it only a dream?
Raggedy Ann's mouth,

Now looked closed in a smile.
I really do dream, once in a while.
But when we're asleep,
Do toys really play?
Must we sit them down,
And tell them to stay?
If the answer is yes,
I know what I'll do.
In the toy box they will go,
Until daylight peeks through.
Laugh if you want but wait till tonight,
When you sleep with your toys.
And turn out the light!

When she finished reading her poem, everyone clapped, even the teacher. When everyone had read their poems, Mrs. Terry stood and in a soft voice she said, "I have never been so pleased with a class! You have gone above and beyond my expectations.

Moving along, that year seemed special. We really liked the school and the teachers. Our subjects were a little hard but as you know life doesn't always come easy.

Chapter Twenty

Living And Learning

I remember 8th grade and all the ups and downs. Some days all goes well, and you are up. The next day you have a test, and you are down. That is living. I remember also learning something new and how good that felt. There is joy in learning and doing your best.

We had so many different subjects. Reading was no longer just reading for enjoyment. We discussed the plot of the story, the theme, and the characters in fiction.

Our writing involved several steps. After deciding what we would write about and getting started, we sometimes had to look back and revise it, maybe several times. I tore up a lot of paper that year!

Social Studies and History gave us a better look at the world and the past. We understood more of the sacrifices that the armed forces had made to keep our country free. I, for one, look at the flag that flies over our land with more respect.

I really don't want to talk about math because I still struggle and perhaps always will. My dad keeps saying, practice makes perfect. I will give you an idea of what it was about that year.

We found the volume of three-dimensional shapes, including cones, spheres, and cylinders. We learned about square roots. We also made charts and graphs to explain patterns in the data. Enough, enough, and too much about math!

Let me fill you in about my favorite subject!!! I had a typing class. This made my day! Learning to type was not really easy, but it was fun. I was soon able to complete many of my lessons on our old typewriter at home. I saved the best till last.

My parents told me if I could type 40 words a minute and get an A in this class, they would buy me a computer!! They told me it would be a great help in High School. I did and they did. HAPPY DAY.

I was the first to have a computer among my friends and was happy to let them use it. The second semester of eighth grade was filled with hard work, fun, and friendship.

We had begun to look forward to graduation and high school. Then the unexpected happened. One of our classmates died. A happy, friendly, and talented boy had a sudden heart attack and passed away.

Our graduation was saddened, and many tears were shed as we walked across the stage to receive our diplomas. There was a space left where he would have stood and his name was called out.

A man in the audience stood up. It was his Dad. He walked to the stage and received his son's diploma. I don't think there was a dry eye in the room. The tears fill my eyes even now as I write about it.

Our parents struggled to make the day better for my friends and me. Our families went to lunch together and then we talked about our summer vacation and what we would do.

I turned to Jimmy and John on the way out of the restaurant and said, "Life goes on. We are left with memories and will never forget our friend."

Chapter Twenty-One

Friends Together

As our families had become good friends, we talked about our summer plans. The grownups talked and we three boys listened. Every once in a while, they would ask if we would like to visit this or that place. Every place looked good to us. Like most kids, we just wanted to go!!

After much discussion, John's dad said, "I know your families have been to Washington D.C., but I would really like for John to see our country's capital. Would you like to go there again?"

Jimmy's mom said, "I think that is a good idea. You can never see it all in only one trip." A vote was taken, and everyone agreed that would be fun. So, it was decided, all we had to do was get ready.

The caravan pulled out on Friday, three motorhomes long. Our trip was special because we were together. We visited several places along the way. A few days later we were in Washington D.C.

We parked our motorhomes and rented a large SUV so we could tour the city together. This was the first thing we did. Then everyone was hungry, and we went to a small café and had a nice lunch.

Then the fun began! Our first stop was the Smithsonian National Zoo. Our parents are super smart also, they had sent for passes about a month earlier. I have been to many zoos, but this tops them all. I cannot tell you the names of all the animals we saw. I will name a few. We saw elephants and slurp ants, animals large and small. We saw sea lions catch fish and looked at alligators and lizards. Everyone's favorite was having front row seats watching zookeepers work with animals. And we got to sit down! We left happy and tired, ready for a good's night rest.

The next day we went on a bus tour and learned more about the city.

Our last stop was the Museum of the Bible. We planned to stay most of the day as there were six floors to look at and there was a lot to see. And it costs money to get in! The entrance was made of stained glass showing the creation from Genesis. We ate lunch at a restaurant there and walked our legs off! It was wonderful but everyone was ready to go home.

Our caravan left the next morning for home. The first day was pretty quiet. A few days later we were home and happy. But boys will be boys, and we were up and at it the next morning.

We met in Jimmy's back yard to talk about the trip and about the next year in school. This was going to be another new start.

Chapter Twenty-Two

High School

To tell you the truth, we were all worried! Did we cry? Not in front of each other, but I shed a few tears that night thinking about math. Back to our talk! I asked Jimmy how he felt about being called Jimmy in high school. He said, "I hadn't thought about it, but it does sound like a little kid." I told him I felt the same way about my name.

We turned to John and asked him what he thought about our changing to Tim and Jim. I have never heard John laugh like that! When he stopped laughing, he told us this, "before I moved to this town, I was called Johnny and then I changed it to John. After we quit laughing the change was made. Of course, we had to tell our parents and they said they thought it was a good idea as we were becoming young men.

Chapter Twenty-Three

Three Young Men

We had to think about that statement. Men, we said and looked at each other. We were taller, that was true, but men were different. What makes boys into young men?

As we talked, we came to this conclusion. The first thing was age. But age did not make men like our dads. They were tall, we were getting there. They were smart, we had that, and laughed. They had worked hard to be successful, but how did they start? I told you we were smart, so we did the smart thing. We asked them how they grew to be good men like we knew they were.

Their answer was simple. "We came from a home that surrounded us with love. We were encouraged to always do our best in whatever was before us. It was not always easy, but they had learned the lesson they had taught us. Never give up!" They continued, "we worked hard in school, and it was not always easy. After college we did not start at the top but continued working and following directions. Just like school, it was one step at a time."

Then John's dad said this, "To be a real man you must be kind, and you must have a loving heart. Knowing God and accepting him as your Savior helps you to understand this. All three of you will be real

men!" We all shook hands, and we three young men climbed the ladder again.

Chapter Twenty-Four

A Giant Step

Suddenly it happened. The day we had talked about and thought about was here. We stepped on a new bus with smiles on our faces to greet some of our friends from junior high. They were really smiles of hope, not happiness. We were starting a new beginning. What would it bring? Only time would tell as we began our journey. A quiet group of young ladies and young men stepped down from the bus to meet their future.

Chapter Twenty-Five

School Year Nine

Time moves on and another step up the ladder for three concerned friends. There were so many classrooms in this new school. IT WAS LARGE! We would have to learn to find our way around.

Homeroom and once again we were together. Well, that was a good start. Our instructor looked like a nice older man. He introduced himself as Mr. Jones. His first words were "Welcome to Hoover High School. I will help you succeed and be happy here. This is my twentieth year here and I have enjoyed them all. This is your homeroom and I teach English." After role and the flag salute he passed out maps of the school. This would be a great help. The next was each student's schedule.

"Please feel free to ask any questions and I will try to answer them. We will do no work today. After we pass out the books, we will get acquainted, he quietly stated. "This is a new beginning for you and all the staff want these to be good four years for you. This is your step toward college, so do your best. We can only teach and help when we can, and you must do the work. Trust me, it will all be worth it. What now seems strange will soon be a part of your growing up and becoming young ladies and young men." He also told us, and I quote "A job worth doing is worth doing well."

That could not have been a better start in a new school. Everyone felt welcome and safe. We could do this! One step up at a time.

Chapter Twenty-Six

Not Alone!

Our next period went well as John, and I were together. Of course, it was math!

Having the same work could be a help. What one of us could not understand, maybe the other one did. Then we could help one another. There is an old saying, and it is true. (A trouble shared is a trouble halved) We always had the help of our friend Jim. Our families were also very supportive and helped when they could.

After the first few weeks, once again a tutor was hired to help both of us one evening a week. This began to make a difference. This tutor had a way of explaining so we caught on better. Patience was his rule and he never moved on until he was sure we understood.

This would never be my favorite subject, but at least I was moving along with the class. My fear of a test lessened. I was passing with a C and not a D!

As we left the class we parted. John went to PE, and I went to my music class. My parents had bought me a violin and I had been taking lessons for three years and was ready to join the school orchestra. I had always loved music, especially the old hymns at church.

I was so happy to have this class. It was one of my favorites. I not only learned to play the violin but also the drums! So, it was orchestra and band. Each different and both fun! We had to practice over and over. How many times did our instructor tell us, "Practice makes perfect."

I wanted to say that we would never be perfect, but I didn't. I did not want to burst his bubble!

The next period was P.E. and that went well. Then it was time for lunch, and I was hungry.

Chapter Twenty-Seven

Cafeteria Lunch

I thought lunch was good at Junior High! This was unbelievable, it looked like a mile of food. There were salads, several different meats, all kinds of vegetables, rolls and then the desserts! We could choose a salad, one meat, two vegetables and a roll. We had a choice of one dessert. As well as I can remember the cost was $2.00. Milk went with lunch, or you could buy a soft drink from a machine. Those ladies must have cooked for hours. After eating we talked with friends about their morning. Most of our friends were happy with the classes they had in the new school. Everyone gave a high-five for the lunch. Everyone left full of food and hoping for a happy afternoon.

Only two more classes today.

Chapter twenty-Eight

First Day Ends

Everyone went their own way to the next class saying they would meet at the bus stop.

My next class was World History. I already knew I would like this. I had always loved this subject. I was not prepared for the old history that I did not know anything about. I was also not prepared for all the homework, writing and tests for this class. I still liked it, but it was work! I will always remember one thing the instructor said, "We are history in the making."

I guess everyone has a health class in the ninth grade. I thought, I am healthy, why do I need this class? I found out many things I did not know about staying healthy that year. It is the food you eat, how much you eat, exercise and how much you exercise. We found more about the dangers of alcohol and drugs. I could not believe what I did not know! You must choose wisely to stay healthy. I had been well versed in these things all my life. My mom cooked well, and we ate healthy meals. No one in my family or my friend's families drank liquor. This was a blessing that I did not understand until I listened to some of the students tell of parents with drinking problems.

One boy said in class that his dad would never take a drink because his father and two brothers were alcoholics and talked about the problems it brought to their families. This was when I silently said a prayer of thanks that it wasn't in my family. I also prayed for the boy who shared his story. Everyone left the room quietly and headed for the buses to go home. We had a lot to think about.

Oops! I forgot to tell you about P.E., but I will get to it tomorrow.

Chapter Twenty-Nine

Story Continues

Mr. Jones met us at the door with a smile. Are you ready to get to work?" he said. Everyone said yes and he gave each student a high five as they entered. As we were seated, he asked us to take our books out of our backpacks and read the first story After we completed reading it, we would write a review of the story. We might want to think about the story and perhaps read it again before we began to write was Mr. Jones advice. The paper was to include three items. The first was do you like it and why or why not. The second was do you agree with the author about his findings. The third was, how would you change it.

"Let me be clear about this paper. You can use a computer or typewriter if one is available. IF it is handwritten, the handwriting must be well done! If I have a hard time reading it you will receive an F.

Remember what I said, "I teach, and you work."

This was to be completed and would be our homework for tonight. I wondered how much homework I would have before the day was over.

Then I went to math class. Why was I not surprised when Mr. Stanfield (that was the instructor's name) passed out some worksheets for us to complete in class and some more (3) for homework. Well, I guessed I would be up until midnight doing homework. John was not happy either. Then I thought about an old saying --- "Where there's a will there's a way." I would do my best to complete my work.

My next class was music and I loved it! NO HOMEWORK. Mr. Scott was a very kind instructor. When a mistake was made, he just said, "let's try that over."

My next class was P.E., and I was happy to see Jim and John were both there. It was always fun to have a class together.

It seemed a little unusual for a boy's

class to have a female instructor but we had one before, so it was fine with us. Her name was Mrs. Pratt, and she was a great instructor! She told us baseball was her favorite sport. This was our first sport of the year, and it was great. If the weather was a little too hot, she would call for time out and we had water and 10 minutes rest.

After this class it was time for lunch. In all our high school years, we were never disappointed with it, everything was always delicious.

Chapter Thirty

Smooth Sailing

It seemed like I sailed through the world history class the whole semester. Mrs. Crow was such a nice teacher. She was always smiling and seemed happy to greet each student.

It was not an easy class, there was a lot of work, some homework, and many tests. Her teaching skills helped us to understand the text and she willingly answered all questions. What we were tested on, was only about what we had studied. There were no trick questions. I know you understand that last line!

I almost hated to go to my next class, which was health. It was hard to hear what some of the students were talking about yesterday. There are a lot of problems in some homes. BUT, Miss Johnson, our instructor completely changed the topic.

We watched videos about how and where the fruits and vegetables were grown.

We talked about vitamins and what they were needed for. She told us about her garden and showed some films she had taken. And then the best! She had brought some vine ripened tiny tomatoes and let us eat some. Store bought would never taste as good again.

I told my parents about it, and they said we would have some tomato plants next year in our backyard. I was looking forward to that.

Chapter Thirty-One

Next Semester

The first semester of ninth grade was a learning experience. We had the same instructors and classes all that year except one. Health was a one semester class. We could choose an elective class for the last semester. My choice was woodshop.

On the first day, we only toured the large room. There were large tools and small tools like you find in almost any garage. This was no touch day, only look.

It was explained what each tool could be used for and the necessity of wearing a face shield and gloves.

Then the teacher said, "I have something to tell you, please don't laugh."

"My name is Mr. Woods." And then everyone laughed, even Mr. Woods. What a fitting name for a wood shop teacher!

Before we left, he showed us some samples of what we could make this semester. Most students start with a hiking stick he told us. It is really fun to make. "I have been gathering some straight limbs from my friends who are tree trimmers.

Everyone may have one or if you have one at home, you can bring that." It would be hard to imagine some of the items he showed us that students had made. Of course, some had taken woodshop for all four years of high school.

This was my favorite class of the year. Before it was over, I had made a hiking stick, a key holder, a cube candle holder, a pencil holder and the best of all, a birdhouse.

No more worries about high school. I loved it and I loved learning new things. I even kinda (wrong English,

I meant kind of) liked math. I found out you needed it in woodshop for making many items. I was beginning to see how it would be useful in life.

Another year was ended, vacation was coming, and there were no worries about next year!! Three young men were coming back.

Chapter Thirty-Two

Auto or Train?

What started at the end of last summer was still happening. This was the discussion of what we would do this summer. As we were now young men, we were included in the talks. There were so many places we would like to go, but our parents first thought was the cost of the trip. It seemed every year the trips became more costly.

There was one thing we all agreed on. We wanted to ride on a train. What fun to sight-see on a ride where no one has to drive, and everyone can enjoy the trip. A long trip for nine people was too expensive. The decision was made to take a short trip from Bakersfield to Fresno. We would stay in a hotel and go to a live show that night. One thing was settled, finally.

Where to go next? We had only tried to decide for a year! John, Jim, and I looked at each other, went outside and talked about it. We brought our decision to our parents. It was this. You are the grownups, and you are paying for the trip. Wherever you want to do, we will be happy. We are just blessed to be together. Then we went outside to play catch.

That evening it was settled. We would travel as usual going up the coastline as far as Vancouver, Washington. We would stop at points of interest along the way and spend two weeks just being together and having fun.

The weeks went quickly and with no stress. We did not have to be at a certain place at a certain time.

With another summer over, we were ready to return to school. I had not worried about math all summer.

Chapter Thirty-Three

Return Again

Over the summer, my friends and I had turned 16. The first class we wanted to take was Driver Training. We had requested it last year but did not know if we would be able to get it. It seemed almost everyone wanted to take it. About a week before school was to start, we got our class list in the mail. WE WERE IN!

My thoughts were only about learning to drive as I gazed around the room. Many of the students were girls, I mean young women, and they seemed to have grown up over the summer. And then I spotted her, Eudora. Wow, she was looking better every year. When she saw me looking at her, she turned her head away. It doesn't hurt to look, does it?

I will not bore you with all the classes my friends and I took that year. You remember your high school days and the struggles and blessings.

We were climbing higher, one small step at a time. And then it happened, I looked in the mirror and saw some fuzz on my chin. HAIR! I had been looking for this. Now I could shave like a man, or maybe I would grow a beard.

I do need to tell you a little bit about tenth grade. Besides driver training, I took another year of woodshop. I enjoyed making items of wood and made Christmas things for my family. I made a jewelry box for my mom and a shaving holder for my dad.

These were two fun classes, but also teaching and learning classes. That goes hand in hand. The instructor teaches and the students learn. Sometimes I wondered what I would do after high school. Did I want to go to college? What did I want to do with my life. I made an appointment with our school counselor.

The first question he asked me was one I had asked myself. What do you want to do with your life? I hesitated for a minute and then said, "I believe I am being called to be a preacher. I love the Lord and want to serve

Him." The counselor reached over and patted my shoulder and said, "I have never been happier in my job than you have made me today, we will work together to select the right classes for you in your junior and senior year and search for the right college." He told me it was critical to continue to make excellent grades as colleges look at transcripts. He asked if I had told my parents about becoming a preacher. I said that I hadn't, and he told me to talk to them and we would talk later.

I went home and after dinner I told my parents about my decision. They were happy that I had made this my goal in life, and they would pray that the Lord would use me to further His work.

I began working on Saturdays at a homeless shelter preparing and serving meals. This was a lifestyle I had never seen before. I realized that I had led a sheltered life, and everyone did not have the same opportunities as I had. My eyes were being opened to the world as it really was.

I was learning a lot about life, in school and out. My choices would affect my future. Needless to say, my grades went up to all A's and only one B, which was a step up in math.

Chemistry, world history, language arts and geometry, driver training, wood shop and music were my classes. All I will say is that I did my best.

My counselor suggested that as part of the summer my family and I could visit some colleges that I was interested in.

I cannot leave tenth grade without telling you about the after-school class. Almost unbelievable. There was going to be a ballroom dancing class. It was open to all students in tenth grade. We would have to have permission from parents and a way to get home as school busses would not be available. Many of my friends were going, including Tim and John. We set it up with our parents so they could take turns picking us up. It was so cool!

First, we lined up and the teacher showed us the steps and we tried to do them.

Waltz steps were the first ones we tried. The boys were lined up on one side and the girls on the other. You are doing very well the instructor said. "Now, I want you to try it with a partner." RIGHT NOW? I said before I could stop myself. "Yes, the first five boys in line, please walk to the girl's line and politely ask a girl if she would like to dance.

    The first boy walked right over to Eudora and asked her, and she accepted. I wished I had been first in line. The class lasted for four weeks, and I did get to dance with her.

Chapter Thirty-Four

Looking

For the first time, our families were not going on a trip together. Each family would spend the first week visiting colleges which would suit their sons. Tim had decided he wanted to be a doctor and John wanted to be a teacher. Different colleges were going to be looked at. Our friendships were getting closer, and our futures seemed to be moving us apart. The first day of vacation we three young men met in my backyard and talked about the future.

Nothing would or could change our friendship. We were friends for life.

The second week our families got together for dinner and talked about the future and colleges for their sons. After this discussion, they talked about spending some time together. John's mom said, "Why don't we rent a house for a week at Lake Arrowhead. We could swim and fish and take hikes and just spend time together." We had become more than friends, we felt like families. It was decided, we would go to Lake Arrowhead. We had a great time!

After we got home, I told my parents that I was going to find a summer job. I found work at a local supermarket and began to stock shelves. It felt so good to become a young man with a future before him.

School would be starting soon, and it was time to shop for clothes. I think I had grown two inches that year and my pants were all too short. Mom and I looked, and I tried on different items, and we picked some out. Was mom in for a surprise. I had been saving my money and opened a bank account. The girl totaled the items and mom opened her purse to take out the money and I pulled out my checkbook and wrote a check for the amount. Mom just looked at me and didn't say anything, until we got home. "Why did you do that?" she asked.

"Mom, I said, I will soon finish high school and be off to college. I need to grow up and begin to take responsibility for myself. Clothes are just a part of it, I am also saving for a car so I can drive where I need to go. I just want to do my part; you also have a life and I want you to be able to save for your retirement. I have already decided that I will have a part time job when I go to college to help with the expense.

My counselor also said we should look into scholarships to help with tuition. Later that evening, mom told my dad what I had said. He came to my room, gave me a hug, and said that I had become a fine young man.

Chapter Thirty-Five

Junior Year

So many good years to remember. My junior year was a really great one. I went out for baseball and was selected for the team. I would like to have been the pitcher, but John was better, and I ended up on second base.

Our first game was at our school, and we won 15 to 5. The cheerleaders cheered, the band played, and the crowd went wild. Did I tell you this? Eudora was one of the cheerleaders and did she look good. Of course, they all did but I thought she outshined them all.

I had all the classes which were required and Tim, John, and I decided to have a fun class together. You are not going to believe this; we took a cooking class and were in there with 32 girls. The teacher asked the first day if we were sure we were in the right class and we answered yes. Would I do this again? You bet I would. I learned to cook a few things and learned that no one was going to clean up after me. We were teased by some of our friends but the second semester, ten boys took the class!

Chapter Thirty-Six

Prom Night

We were quickly growing up to be young men. Taller, more muscular. and looking more at the girls. We talked about the prom that was coming up. We knew how to dance, and it sounded like fun. We were seventeen and had been on a few dates. Should we, could we ask a girl to the prom. The first thing we had to do was talk to our parents about it. Please help us with this was what we said. After they finished laughing, they said that of course we should go. "You better find a girl first," they said, and then laughed some more.

 I caught up with Eudora between classes and asked her if she would go to the prom with me. She smiled and said that she would love to. It was done. What else did I have to do to get ready? Mom said I would have to purchase a corsage and suggested one Eudora could wear on her wrist. She also said I needed a new suit as the pants were too short on my old (one and only) one. "Should it be black, brown, or gray?" she asked. What did it matter? I responded with, I guess black, I don't know, does it matter?" Dad broke in and said, "I think it should be black. Now, I will rent a limousine to take you to the dance. It will pick you up after the dance is over and take your date home."

After mom left the room, dad said we needed to have a talk. Then he asked me a question. "How serious is it between you and Eudora? She is the only girl you ever talk about." I looked at him with surprise. "She is my girlfriend, and we are going steady. I like her a lot." My dad said that she was a wonderful girl, but I had a lot of years ahead of me before I could plan a life with a mate. He was so serious, not smiling. "You have to be careful my son, you have another year of high school and then you will be away at college for four. That will be the time to plan for the future." That was the end of the conversation, but it gave me a lot to think about.

I took Eudora to the prom, and we had a wonderful time. I kissed her at her door and said I would see her at school. I was only seventeen, but I knew in my heart that she was the girl for me, and I hoped the next few years would go quickly.

Chapter Thirty-Seven

Flying High

My junior year was over, and I had turned eighteen. Not a child and not quite a man. I often wondered what my future would hold. Would I be ready for college after my last year of high school? Which college would I choose. What did the Lord have planned for me?

But now it was time for family planning for summer. Once again three families would travel together. We would start in a week and the plans were already made. We were going to travel to Alaska. This summer we were going to fly to Seattle, Washington and then take a cruise. It sounded like so much fun. Our parents had been saving all year for this trip as it would be expensive. This would be special as next summer three young men would be preparing for college.

First flight and first cruise for my two friends and me. This was so exciting I could hardly wait for the next day which was when we would be leaving.

I will tell you this. It was the best vacation I had ever had and that is saying a lot. I loved flying! Then, I saw the ship. It was huge and beautiful. We did not have outside cabins, they were too expensive, but we were only going to sleep in them, so they were fine. Another good thing about the trip was that meals were included. We met the captain of the ship, and he entertained us with stories of other voyages. He told us he hoped we would see some whales on our voyage. We hoped so too.

This was the trip of a lifetime. It was not long until we spotted ice bergs. On one was a huge brown bear. He or she just watched us like he had seen it all before.

Skagway, Sitka, and Ketchikan were some of our stops. At one stop we panned for gold and found a few flakes. The shops were the most fun for the moms. They bought so many souvenirs they had to buy a small suitcase to hold them all.

Was it cold? When we were sailing it was cold in the mornings, especially if the wind was blowing. Much of the time our parents were having a good time inside, but the three musketeers were outside enjoying the sights. I really hated that they missed seeing a whale jump out of the water close to the ship.

However, it wasn't long until an announcement was made over the loudspeaker, Whales on the starboard side. Our folks were the first ones out. So many sights, so many adventures, so much fun, and a trip we will never forget.

After we returned home, all our parents said, "It was worth every penny we spent!"

Chapter Thirty-Eight

Senior Year - Never An End

This will be a hard chapter for me to write. My friends and I would be going separate ways after our senior year. We were pretty quiet as we rode the bus the first day. Sometimes growing up is hard.

But that is in the future so I will tell you about our last year in high school.

Once again Jim, John and I had the first period class together. As we each went to our next class, we said we would meet for lunch and share our mornings. We did this the whole year and spent the bus ride home talking about our day.

We talked about the good and the not so good. Most of it was about the good. Our work was hard, but we were used to that and always did our best.

Each of us wanted to see a report card with all A's. John and Jim made it the first semester, but I got one B. The last semester I did it, for the first time in my life I received all A's. Our dedication to our school work had paid off. I did not feel super smart but super blessed.

I had been guided by loving parents, helping me feel secure with good friends, and encouraged to always try hard and do my best.

Once again it was time for the prom. This was special as it was our senior prom. Our last one in high school. Tim and his girlfriend Sally were chosen to be Queen and King of the prom.

They danced the first dance alone on the dance floor and I could see tears drop from Sally's eyes. It was a great evening.

The time was passing quickly, and June was almost here, Graduation was looming near. Everyone was happy and a little sad as a part of our lives were ending. Many would drift away and continue their lives elsewhere.

I knew that the three musketeers would be separated for the first time. I knew another old saying that I shared with them. "The way to a friend's house is never long."

We vowed to keep in touch by phone or writing to each other no matter how busy we were.

I realized then how important friendships are and the value they bring into your life. It would be fun to see who wrote or called first.

Chapter Thirty-Nine

GRADUATION

The time had finally come. Thirteen years of our life in school was ending. Some would continue to college, and some would begin new jobs. A new life was beginning.

Scholarships were many and my friends and I received a few. All of our families were so proud of us.

John. He was the valedictorian! He was usually a man of few words but not this night. His speech was the finest. He spoke of the opportunities that education gave each student.

The staff was given the highest credit for a job well done. It was not long, but it said what each of us would like to say.

This was the best school, the best instructors, and the best staff according to John. We all agreed.

As the names were called the student walked slowly across the stage, shook the President's hand, received his or her diploma, and walked down the steps to the future. We were young and we were quickly becoming men and women.

On Saturday morning, Eudora and her parents came for a visit. We needed to talk to everyone about our future. We were clear about what we wanted ours to be. We were in love and would wait until we finished college to marry.

We wanted their blessings on our plans. I believe they were relieved that we were willing to wait and hugged and kissed us and gave us their blessings. Four years is a long time, but this too will pass.

Before I left for college, I gave Eudora a poem I had written. I would like to share it with you.

Eudora

Eudora is nice, Eudora is sweet,

Unless, of course, we happen to meet.

Her eyes open wide,

Her hands become fists.

She reaches to hit me,
But somehow, it's a miss.
I'm only eleven,
And she's so cool.
Why is she angry,
When I follow her to school?
I'll love her forever,
Why can't she see?
Someday it will be,
Eudora and me.

Eudora is nineteen,
Eudora is sweet.
Until of course,
We happen to meet.
Her eyes open wide,
Her hands reach for mine.
This sure is different,
Than when she was nine.
I'm twenty-one now,

And my love is still strong.

In my arms forever,

Is where she belongs.

Time makes a difference,

As you can see.

Now and forever,

It's Eudora and me.

EPILOGUE

This book, Timmy Climbs Higher, is my last book of the How Timmy Grew Series.

I can only say, I have loved writing these books. Don't believe that this is the end of Timmy because there are thousands of Timmy's in our world who need our love and support.

The children in my books were secure and happy. In the real world it is not always like that.

Everyone can't give their children all the things that money can buy. They can all give them something much better - Love.

I hope the message of these three books was clear, that Timmy was not successful because of the worldly things in his life. Timmy was successful because of the love, support, understanding, encouragement and help he received from his family. This gave him the desire and the confidence to succeed.

You, my readers, have blessed me with your love and support. Is the next book ready yet? How is Timmy doing? What educational programs was he in now? These were questions I heard from my friends and family.

What a joy. I hope I have blessed you with my fictional families.

May God bless you as you travel through life.

My Thank You

I give thanks to the Lord for allowing me to live long enough to complete this series. And the talent to write it. Without his love, I am nothing.

Once again, my thank you goes to Scott and Hazel Brown and Nova Publishing Co. Thank you for your encouragement and especially your patience!

There are a multitude of family and friends whom I would like to list individually but that would make the thank you page longer than the book!!

Thank you everyone for your prayers and encouragement. God bless you.

Love, Rose

Made in United States
Orlando, FL
17 June 2023